The Catholic Kid's Guide to STEWARDSHIP

Elizabeth M. Johnson

TWENTY-THIRD PUBLICATIONS
 185 WILLOW STREET • PO BOX 180 • MYSTIC, CT 06355
TEL: 1-800-321-0411 • FAX: 1-800-572-0788
Bayard E-MAIL: ttpubs@aol.com • www.twentythirdpublications.com

Twenty-Third Publications
A Division of Bayard
185 Willow Street
P.O. Box 180
Mystic, CT 06355
(860) 536-2611 or (800) 321-0411
www.twentythirdpublications.com
ISBN:1-58595-292-3

Acknowledgments

My thanks to everyone who helped to make this book possible: to the young Catholics who are shining examples of what it means to be stewards of God's gifts; to the Catholic newspaper editors, diocesan directors of stewardship, parish directors of religious education, Catholic school principals, and parents who shared with me the stories of so many extraordinary kids; to my friend, Bob Bittner, for encouraging me throughout the writing process; to my parents, Steve and Fran Welch, for nurturing my gift for writing; and, most of all, to my dear husband Jay and to my terrific kids—Matthew, Christopher, Gregory, and Catherine—for inspiring me, supporting me, and believing in me every step of the way.

Contents

A Note to Parents, Teachers, and Catechists

The Catholic Kid's Guide to Stewardship is written for kids. It introduces them to the idea of Christian stewardship, and shows them what kids just like them are doing to serve God by serving others. You may want to read along and discuss the ideas in the book with them.

Throughout the book are places where you can join in to help the child or children in your life learn more. Each chapter includes "Read All about It" sections that direct the reader to Scripture passages mentioned in the book. There are also sections called "A Note to Parents, Teachers, and Catechists" in each chapter that offer ideas for activities to do together. These will help children practice the concepts they learned in the text.

I'm Just a Kid! What Can I Do?

Let no one despise your youth, but set the believers an example. —1 Timothy 4:12

Sagen Woolery, a second-grader in Georgia, wanted to feed hungry kids in her town by starting a summer lunch program. However, it wasn't easy for her to put her idea into action. When Sagen's mother introduced her to a man at their church who ran a local soup kitchen, he said that Sagen was too young to do a project like that. Sagen kept asking him for help again and again. Finally he couldn't ignore her any more. After two years, he agreed to help her make her dream come true. By the end of the summer, Sagen and her team of peers had made lunches for more than 300 needy children. Sagen didn't let anyone tell her she was "too young" to serve others. Sagen knew she wasn't too young to be a follower of Jesus.

What does Jesus want his followers to do? Here is what he says:

"Come, you that are blessed by my Father, inherit the kingdom prepared for you from the foundation of the world; for I was hungry and you gave me food, I was thirsty and you gave me something to drink, I was a stranger and you welcomed me, I was naked and you gave me clothing, I was sick and you took care of me, I was in prison and you visited me." Then the righteous will answer him, "Lord, when was it that we saw you hungry and gave you food, or thirsty and gave you something to drink? And when was it that we saw you a stranger and welcomed you, or naked and gave you clothing? And when was it that we saw you sick or in prison and visited you?" And the king will answer them, "Truly I tell you, just as you did it to one of the least of these who are members of my family, you did it to me." (Matthew 25:34–40)

That seems like a lot to ask of anyone, even grown-ups. But is Jesus just speaking to grown-ups? No. If you are a follower of Jesus, then these words are meant for you, too. Before you say, "But that's impossible! I'm just a kid," remember that Jesus said, "With God, nothing is impossible." He also said, "Let the children come to me." Jesus loved children, and even told his followers that they must become like children to enter the kingdom of heaven.

READ ALL ABOUT IT · READ ALL ABOUT IT · READ ALL ABOUT IT · READ ALL ABOUT IT

You can read what Jesus said about children in your Bible. Have an adult help you find the following Scripture passages:

Matthew 18:1–4
Mark 10:13–16
Luke 18:15–17

Doing what Jesus asked his followers to do is part of a bigger idea called "stewardship." You may have heard that word at church and wondered what it meant. A steward is a person who takes care of something that belongs to someone else. As Christians, we believe that everything we have comes from God. God has asked us to take care of what he has given us and to use it wisely.

What are some of the things God has given us? God has given us our lives, our senses, our talents, and our brains. God has given us our parents, families, friends, and teachers. God has given us food to eat, air to breathe, water to drink, and nature to enjoy. Above all, God has given us his Son, Jesus Christ, to love us and to give his life for us. We have a lot to thank God for. We can show our thanks by caring for all the gifts God has given us and by using them in ways that make God happy. That's what stewardship is about.

Stewardship is more than just doing good deeds, although that is part of it. Stewardship is also the attitude behind those deeds. If you give some of your toys to the Christmas toy drive at church, but pout and whine and throw a fit about it, that's not stewardship. If you rake the leaves in your neighbor's yard just because you want to get five dollars from her, that's not stewardship. There's nothing wrong with doing a job for pay, but there is a difference between doing a job just as a way to earn money and doing a job also as a way of showing love for God and your neighbor. If you join the children's choir just because you want everyone to hear what a beautiful voice you have, that's not stewardship.

Stewardship says "Thank you, God," not "Look at me." When you give your toys to a poor child, you are saying, "Thank you, God, for giving me a family who gives me toys to play with. I want to make another child happy by sharing my toys with them." When you rake the yard for your neighbor, you are saying, "Thank you, God, for giving me a strong body. Thank you for giving me a friendly neighbor. I want to use my strength to help her and show how much I like her." When you sing in the choir, you are saying, "Thank you, God, for giving me the gift of a beautiful voice. I want to use my voice to praise you and to share your message with others."

Christian stewardship is usually divided into three areas: time, talent, and treasure. You may think you don't have any of these things to share, but you do! Here are a few examples of how you can share your time, talent, and treasure.

Time

One of the best ways you can use your time is to pray. Praying is spending time with God—a very good use of your time. You can pray alone, with your family, or at church. You can pray to thank God, to ask God's help with problems in your own life, or to ask for help for others. Other ways to give your time are:

- taking care of a younger brother or sister;
- talking with a grandparent or older person;
- visiting a sick friend;
- helping a classmate with homework;
- doing what your parents ask you to do around the house;
- taking part at Mass, in religious education, and in special parish celebrations.

You don't need any special skills to do these things—you just need to give yourself and some of your time.

Elizabeth Card, an eighth-grader from Joplin, Missouri, shares her time by visiting Alzheimer's patients at a local nursing home. Students at St. Teresa's School in Austin, Texas, visit children in an orphanage in Mexico. Allison and Chanelle Tischler of Austin, Texas, pray for and send cards to men who are studying to become priests.

Time is a gift from God. The choices we make about how we spend our time can be an act of stewardship. Will you spend an hour watching TV or helping your sister learn to tie her shoes? Will you choose

READ ALL ABOUT IT · READ ALL ABOUT IT · READ ALL ABOUT IT · READ ALL ABOUT IT

A "mite" is a small bit. You can read the gospel passage of The Widow's Mite in Mark 12:41–44 or Luke 21:1–4.

to play a video game or help your mother make brownies for the parish bake sale? Will you gossip about the other kids at school or pray for them? Ask yourself: am I filling my hours with activities that please God and help others? When you are, you are practicing stewardship of time.

Talent

Everyone has at least one talent. Everyone has gifts. Sure, you may not hit a baseball like Sammy Sosa, sing like LeeAnn Rimes, or act like Frankie Muniz, but not every person's talent is a blockbuster. Talent doesn't mean being the best at something. Anything we can do, even if we aren't the best at it, is a talent given to us by God.

What are your talents?

• Are you a good reader? You can share that talent by reading to a younger sibling or to an elderly person in a nursing home.

• Are you a good cook? How about baking some cookies for holiday dinners for the needy?

• Do you like to draw? Make a poster for the parish food drive, or make Valentine cards to send to soldiers overseas.

• Do you make friends easily? You can share your talent by welcoming a new kid at your school.

• Do you like to sing? Perhaps there's a place for you in the children's choir.

• Do you have good organizational skills? The local food pantry might need your help sorting through canned goods and stocking the shelves. A disabled neighbor might appreciate your help with yard work.

Whatever you do well, whatever makes you happy when you do it, that's your gift. The best way you can thank God for your gifts is to use them and share them with others. That way, you serve God with the gifts God has given you.

Britten Megargle of Holy Spirit Parish in Hamburg, Michigan, uses her talent for sewing to make stuffed animals from old clothing. She sells the toys to raise money for a local crisis pregnancy center. Nicole and Zack Gomolski of Idaho, have a talent for gardening, so they grow crops of okra and pumpkins to share with their neighbors. William Jude of Gilford, New Hampshire, uses his talent as a writer to be a pen pal with a child his family sponsors through the Christian Foundation for Children and Aging.

Treasure

You may not think you have much treasure, but whatever you have in money and material possessions is your "treasure." Treasure is not the loot pirates collect, but rather, the resources we have. Remember the widow in the gospel story who had only two small coins to put in the collection box? Jesus said that her small offering was worth more than the larger amounts other people were giving because it was all she had, and she gave it from her heart. That was her treasure.

Now, God isn't asking you to give all of your money and things away. However, God does invite you to be generous with what you have and also to make wise use of what you keep. How can you do this? One way is by tithing, which means giving ten percent (10%)of what you have to the church or to charity. Ten percent is really not a lot. If you get one dollar for allowance, 10% is only one dime; if you get five dollars, 10% is fifty cents—about the cost of a candy bar. You might want to set up a three-jar system for dividing up the money you get for allowance, chores, gifts, and so on. One jar can be for church and charity, one jar can be for saving up for something special, and one jar can be for spending.

Other ways to share your treasure—or resources—include giving your outgrown clothes to a clothing drive, St. Vincent de Paul, the Salvation Army, or Goodwill. You can also sort through your toys before birthdays and Christmas to give away toys and games you no longer play with. Another treasure you and your family have is recyclable goods. As the saying goes, "One person's trash is another's treasure." When you recycle your newspapers, cans, plastics, and bottles, you help protect the earth (one of God's greatest gifts to us), and you help preserve natural resources by letting companies turn your trash into new products.

A NOTE TO PARENTS, TEACHERS, AND CATECHISTS • A NOTE TO PARENTS, TEACHERS, AND CATECHISTS •

You can help children discover their gifts of time, talent, and treasure. Talk with them about what you and they see as their gifts. Help them make a poster showing how they can use these gifts to honor God and serve other people.

Madison Etzler, a five-year-old in Hallettsville, Texas, donates one-third of any money she gets to charity. Hanna Butler of Falls River Center, Kentucky, asked friends who came to her sixth birthday party to bring canned food instead of presents. Alex Pietrasiuk, a fifth-grader at St. Francis School, Ann Arbor, Michigan, also used his birthday to help others. He asked friends to bring school materials for a school in a poor neighborhood where the kids didn't have supplies to start the school year.

You see, stewardship doesn't have to be hard. You've probably realized by now that you are already practicing stewardship. Now that you know what stewardship is, you can begin to do even more. Thank God for his gifts and find ways to use them in God's service to help others. A good way to begin is by praying this stewardship prayer from the Diocese of Charlotte, North Carolina:

STEWARDSHIP PRAYER

Dear God,

I thank you for everything you have given me. My gifts of time and talents are precious; help me use them to do your will. Please help me realize that I need to share all of my gifts with the Church and others. Help me be generous, forgiving, and holy. I offer you this day all I think, and do, and say. With the help of Jesus, your Son, I will try to love everyone. Amen.

Chapter 2

Kids Can
...Feed the Hungry

There is a boy here who has five barley loaves and two fish. —John 6:9

If you've ever tried to break one cookie into lots of pieces to share with friends, you know it doesn't go very far. You end up wishing there was some way to make sure everybody could get a whole cookie—or even more—instead of just a bite. Jesus' friends felt that way one day when they were out with him, sharing the Good News of God's kingdom. After Jesus preached to a group of thousands of people, his disciples wanted to send everyone home. They didn't know

READ ALL ABOUT IT · READ ALL ABOUT IT · READ ALL ABOUT IT · READ ALL ABOUT IT · READ ALL ABOUT IT

The story of how Jesus fed 5,000 people appears in each of the four gospels. You can read the story in your Bible:
Matthew 14:13–21
Mark 6:34–44
Luke 9:11–17
John 6:1–13

how they would be able to feed everybody. One boy offered to share his own meal—some bread and fish—even though it wouldn't go very far in that big crowd. Five loaves and a couple of dried fish doesn't sound like much, but when the boy shared them with Jesus, the loaves and fish fed 5,000 people—with twelve baskets left over! That's the cool thing about stewardship. God takes our gifts, no matter how small, and does great things with them.

In Matthew 25:35, Jesus says that feeding the hungry is the first way he will know his followers at the end of time. Why should we feed the hungry? Do you remember the last time you were

A NOTE TO PARENTS, TEACHERS, AND CATECHISTS • A NOTE TO PARENTS, TEACHERS, AND CATECHISTS •

Go shopping together to find examples of your favorite foods. Talk about how God provides for our needs by giving us a variety of foods. Take some of the food you buy and share it with someone else—a neighbor, family members, or a food bank.

hungry? Probably all you could think about was food. You may have been grouchy and not very nice to other people. You didn't care about anything else but getting something to eat. God wants people to be happy. God wants them to be able to enjoy all of the good things he has planned for them. Hungry people can't do that, because all they can think about is being hungry.

God made a world full of good things to eat: sweet fruits and berries, crunchy vegetables, milk, grains, and animals for meat. However, not everyone can enjoy God's gifts of food. Some people don't have enough money to buy food. Some people can't get out to the store to buy food. Other people, because they are elderly or handicapped, have a hard time fixing meals for themselves and their families. Some people live in parts of the world where it's hard to grow food. When we feed the hungry, we help other people enjoy God's gifts of food. We say, "Thank you, God," for the food he gives us.

God asks us to share this gift of food. In the Bible, food and sharing are often found together. Families gather around the table, friends come together for a festival, and people spend time together celebrating or visiting.

READ ALL ABOUT IT · READ ALL ABOUT IT · READ ALL ABOUT IT · READ ALL ABOUT IT · READ ALL ABOUT IT · READ ALL ABOUT IT ·

You know the story of Jesus' last supper.
Read about it in the Bible:
Matthew 26:26–30
Mark 14:22–26
Luke 22:14–20

Jesus shared meals with his followers and had dinner with friends and strangers so he could tell them about his Father's kingdom. Jesus enjoyed eating and visiting with his friends Mary and Martha. Even when he fed the 5,000, Jesus had the people sit down together in groups.

Jesus' last supper was a meal shared with his best friends. This meal is at the heart of our Catholic celebration of Jesus' love for us. We celebrate that meal at Mass when we share Eucharist with our parish family. God knows that people are hungry for friendship and love as much as they are hungry for food. When we feed the hungry, we also share ourselves and our time.

Because God has given us gifts of good food, family, and friendship, we try to show our thanks for those gifts by sharing them with others. As Christian stewards, feeding the hungry is one way we can share those gifts.

Can-Do Kids

Kids are answering Jesus' call to feed the hungry in many ways. Meet Dan and Betsy, Christopher, and the James and Debner girls.

Ending Hunger—One Turkey at a Time

"It's not Thanksgiving without turkey!" Dan Nally cried. It was 1996, and he had just watched a TV news report that said the Greater Boston Food Bank was short 5,000 turkeys to give to needy people at Thanksgiving. "That's just wrong," nine-year-old Dan told his little sister, Betsy. "We've got to help."

Dan and Betsy's mom offered to buy a couple of extra turkeys when she went to the store, but Dan and Betsy had bigger plans. The brother and sister colored fliers that they stuffed in mailboxes in their Westwood, Massachusetts, neighborhood. They collected thirty-six turkeys for the food bank. "It felt really good to be able to help," Dan said.

The next year, neighbors asked Dan and Betsy if they were going to collect turkeys again. Sure, the kids said. They called their collection "Turkeys 'R Us." This time, they took fliers to local schools, businesses, and churches. Their parish, St. Denis Catholic Church, put an announcement in the bulletin and donated money to buy turkeys. That year, Dan and Betsy collected 365 turkeys. As they continued their project, more and more people began to donate. There were so many turkeys that the Food Bank sent a refrigerated truck to the Nally's home to make daily pick-ups.

In 2000, talk show host Oprah Winfrey heard about the work Dan and Betsy were doing to feed the hungry, and she invited them to visit her show. She had another surprise guest—Jim Perdue, president of Perdue Farms, a company that sells chickens and turkeys. He told the kids he was going to donate 1,000 turkeys! He also told them that they could buy turkeys from his company for less than they could buy turkeys from the grocery store. That way, when people gave money instead of a turkey, they could buy even more turkeys. In 2002, Dan and Betsy collected more than 6,350 turkeys for needy families. They also expanded their program beyond Boston and changed the name of their group to Turkeys 4 America.

Dan and Betsy don't do all of this work alone. They started a contest for schools called the Turkeys 4 America Challenge. Schools compete to see which one can collect the most turkeys for the food bank. The winning school gets a prize and is honored on the kids' website, www.turkeys4america.org. Dan and Betsy have also posted a list of questions and answers on their website to help other kids start local turkey collection programs.

"Turkeys 4 America isn't about having the most turkeys in Boston. It's about ending hunger," Dan said. "We just want to make sure everyone gets a turkey for Thanksgiving."

Baking the Christmas Spirit into Every Cookie

What could be better than baking dozens of Christmas cookies? Baking them to share with others! That's what nine-year-old Chris Johnson learned when he spent a December weekend making cookies for holiday meals served by the Lansing, Michigan chapter of the Volunteers of America.

Chris loves to cook and bake. When his mom heard a radio ad asking for volunteers to make cookies for Christmas dinners for the homebound, disabled, and elderly people in the community, she asked Chris if he'd like to help out. He liked the idea and started planning what they would make. He decided on chocolate chip cookies and oatmeal raisin cookies—two of his favorites.

Chris, a parishioner at St. Casimir Church in Lansing, had taken part in food drives sponsored by the parish for Easter, Thanksgiving, and Christmas, but this was different. "It's more personal to make something yourself than just to take some cans or boxes off the shelf and bring them to church," he explained. "It's more fun, too."

Chris and his mom spent one Saturday afternoon mixing, baking, and packing eight dozen cookies. When they delivered them to the Volunteers of America office, the volunteer manager told them that the cookies they made would be added to other cookie donations to create plates of assorted cookies. These dessert plates would become part of the Christmas dinners that were delivered to people who would be spending Christmas alone or who couldn't make their own Christmas dinners. Christopher's cookies, she said, would be enjoyed by many people. Chris has suggested that his family make cookie-baking a new Christmas tradition.

Brown Bag Lunches Packed with Love

In Austin, Texas, the James family and the Debner family have made it their mission to feed the hungry by packing sack lunches that are handed out to homeless laborers. The James sisters (fourteen-year-old Meghan, twelve-year-old Ashley, nine-year-old Kristen, and six-year-old Rebekah) and the Debner sisters (eleven-year-old Kelsey, nine-year-old Emily, seven-year-old Stacey, and four-year-old Julie) are homeschooled by their parents, who include Christian service as part of their girls' education.

For the past five years, the girls have gotten together every other week to put food bought by the St. Vincent de Paul Society into paper bags.

"When we pack the lunches for the day laborers, we pack soda, peanut crackers, raisins, Vienna sausages, and cookies," explained Kelsey Debner. "We set everything out in an assembly line and work together. Then we take them to the Mary House Catholic Worker. Lynn is the head of the Catholic Workers there, and she takes them to the work corner for the day laborers."

Even the youngest girls can help with this job, because there are no sandwiches to make—only prepackaged food to sort and pack. Stacey Debner was only two years old when her family began making lunches for the homeless. Now at age seven, she's a real pro at her job. "Even though I'm young, I can still do something that really helps people," she said.

With her sisters and her friends, Ashley James has fed around 15,000 people during a five-year period. "It's great to be able to take time out to feed the hungry," she said. "It's good to know that someone who has no food will get a lunch that I made," added her sister, Kristen.

Idea Starters

What can you do to feed the hungry? There are as many answers as there are kids. Here are some ideas to get you started.

Who is hungry? Take a look around. Do you know anyone who is hungry? For some kids, it may be your little brother or sister who can't reach the cupboard or the fridge yet. You could be a big help to your mom or dad by getting snacks or breakfast for your younger siblings. Do you have a neighbor or relative who is older, or handicapped, or homebound? That person might like some homemade cookies, a loaf of banana bread, or even a nice, simple dinner.

Your parents, teachers, or religious education instructors can help you find ways to aid the hungry. Ask them where you can find information about groups that are feeding the hungry. Does your parish or diocese have a food pantry that needs donations? Is a community center looking for volunteers to serve meals to people who go there for lunch? Social service agencies of both church and community, such as Volunteers of America, Meals on Wheels, Catholic Charities, Catholic Extension Society, and the Catholic Campaign for Human Development, reach out to feed the hungry. Give them a call and ask what you can do.

You can learn about hungry people in other countries and how you can help them by visiting the websites for Food for the Poor (www.foodforthepoor.org) and Heifer International (www.heifer.org). Through the donations of people of all denominations, Heifer International provides plants and farm animals to people in the United States and developing countries so they can have food for their families and also earn money to improve their families' living conditions. Food for the Poor helps the poorest of the poor in Latin America and the Caribbean, using donations to buy rice and beans and milk, as well as supplying shelter and medical help. You can even help contribute food for the hungry by going to The Hunger Site (www.thehungersite.org) and clicking once a day to give a cup of rice to a hungry person.

What do you like to do? Do you enjoy cooking or baking, like Chris Johnson? Maybe you'd like to spend some time in the kitchen making some special goodies to give away. Are you a good organizer, like Dan Nally? You can use your talents to gather a group of friends who will collect canned goods or pack holiday baskets. Do you like to grow things? Maybe you could start a vegetable garden or teach others how to garden so they can grow their own food. Do you like being with people? Serving meals at a soup kitchen may be the right way for you to help feed the hungry.

To get even more ideas, see Chapter 9, "Stewardship Resources."

STEWARDSHIP PRAYER
Feeding the Hungry

Dear God,
You bless us with good things to eat. Open our eyes so we can see the hungry people around us. Help us share your gift of food with them. Help us change our world so everyone will have the food they need to live and grow. We ask this through your Son, Jesus, the Bread of Life. Amen.

Chapter 3

Kids Can...Give Drink to the Thirsty

Whoever gives even a cup of cold water to one of these little ones in the name of a disciple—truly, I tell you, none of these will lose their reward. —Matthew 10:42

Turn on the faucet and fill up a glass with clean, cold water. What could be easier? Yet, for many people in the world getting a drink of clean water is almost impossible. Everything needs water to live—people, animals, and plants. However, even though nearly three-quarters of the earth's surface is covered by water, many people are thirsty. Either they don't have water, or the water they have is too dirty to drink safely.

Water should keep us healthy. Instead, if water is polluted, it can make you sick instead of well. In some countries, children are dying because they don't have clean water to drink. Plants and animals also suffer when water is polluted. When plants and animals become sick or die, then people can't use them for food, which causes even more problems. Water is one of God's greatest gifts, and we need to make sure we take care of it.

Water was important to the people in both the Old and New

Testaments. If you've ever seen pictures of the Holy Land, you know why. Much of the area is desert. When Old Testament writers wanted to express God's goodness, they often wrote about overflowing rivers, refreshing rain showers, and water flowing in the desert. When Moses led the people of Israel out of Egypt and into the desert, God gave them water from a rock so they would not be thirsty. Wells were also important in biblical times. People who didn't have their own wells had to carry large jugs to public wells to get the water they needed for drinking, cooking, and washing. Much time was taken up simply going back and forth to fetch water. In many parts of the world, getting water from a far-off well is still necessary. Women and children can't go to school or do other jobs because they must get water for their families.

READ ALL ABOUT IT · READ ALL ABOUT IT · READ ALL ABOUT IT · READ ALL ABOUT IT

The Bible is filled with passages about water. Here are just two of them. See if you can find others. Exodus 17:1–7 (God brings forth water in the desert), Psalm 65:10–14 (God is praised for his gift of water)

In the New Testament, Jesus used the image of water to describe himself. When he met the Samaritan woman at the well, he told her that he is the "living water." He said that if she drank this water, she would never be thirsty again. Water is also a symbol of healing. Jesus sent the man born blind to wash in the pool of Siloam. He also healed a sick man who had come to the pool at Bethsaida to be healed by the water there. We use water in baptism to show how Christ has washed us clean of our sins and given us new life. When we go to Mass, we bless ourselves with holy water, and we see the priest mix water with wine when he prepares the eucharistic gifts.

When we give drink to people who are thirsty, we help their body, but we also help them enjoy life more. We can also make sure that people have clean water to drink by cleaning up the environment and taking care of the earth.

Can-Do Kids

Clean water, nutritious milk, and healthy trees—see how Ryan, Allison and Chanelle, and the students at St. Olaf's Parish are giving drink to the thirsty.

Clean Water for Africa

When Ryan Hreljac was six years old, his first-grade teacher told him and his classmates about children in Africa who were dying from diseases caused by drinking contaminated water. She told the students that seventy dollars would help build a well that would provide clean water for children in Africa. So Ryan went home and asked his parents for seventy dollars. They told him he could earn the money by doing chores—and he did.

In four months, Ryan had earned seventy dollars, but when he gave his money to WaterCan, a group that works to bring clean water to poor countries, he found out that it would actually take $2,000 to build the well. So he went back home and did more chores. When people heard about what he was doing, they began donating money to help him reach his goal. By the time he was seven years old, he had enough money to build a well.

> **A NOTE TO PARENTS, TEACHERS, AND CATECHISTS**
>
> Help your child find the Holy Land on a map, or find information about the Middle East in magazines or online. Point out the large desert areas, as well as the areas near rivers and lakes where people have settled in cities.

Ryan, a parishioner at Holy Cross Parish in Kemptville, Ontario, Canada, is now thirteen years old. He has made clean water his life's mission. His next fundraising project raised $25,000 to buy a well drill, which makes it easier to build wells, instead of twenty people working for ten days or more to drill a well by hand. In 2000, Ryan went to Africa, where he got to see his well and meet the people in Uganda who were using the well.

A NOTE TO PARENTS, TEACHERS, AND CATECHISTS · A NOTE TO PARENTS, TEACHERS, AND CATECHISTS ·

Read about Jesus' meeting with the Samaritan woman at the well in the gospel of John 4:4–26. John's gospel also has the story of Jesus healing the man at the pool of Bethsaida, John 5:1–9.

Ryan speaks to schools and other groups about the need for clean water in Africa and gets others to help with his projects. In seven years, his organization, Ryan's Well Foundation, has raised more than $800,000 to help people in Africa by providing clean water so that thousands of children can be healthy and happy. Water projects in Uganda, Zimbabwe, Kenya, Malawi, Ethiopia, Nigeria, and Tanzania are "giving drink to the thirsty" thanks to Ryan, who plans to move to Africa when he grows up.

"I want to be a water engineer when I grow up. I want to work until all of Africa has clean water," he said.

Got Goat's Milk?

While most children in the United States drink cow's milk, children in other parts of the world drink milk from goats—when they get any milk at all. Heifer International, an organization that provides farm animals to poor people throughout the world, says that goats are one of the best animals to help people feed their families and earn money for healthcare, food, and education. Goats can live almost anywhere, eat just about anything (even garbage), produce several quarts of milk every day, and give birth to two to three babies a year. This helps families increase their flocks and have even more milk—for drinking and also for making butter, cheese, and yogurt that can be sold or traded.

Children in Charlene Mizenko's fourth grade religious education class at St. Olaf Parish in Poulsbo, Washington, decided they wanted to raise money to buy a goat through Heifer International. One goat costs $120, so they started a program called "Go for the Goat." Kids brought in spare change and also collected soda cans that they took to the recycling center for twenty-one cents a pound. The Knights of Columbus helped out by donating their soda cans, too.

The students invited a speaker to come in and talk to them about how people live in Africa and how goats can make a real difference in the lives of families who own a goat. After hearing the speaker's story, the children wanted to help out more than ever.

The students set up a cardboard thermometer with their goal at the top. Each week, they were able to see how much closer they were to their goal. Other people in the parish made donations, too. By the end of the project, St. Olaf's had raised enough money to buy not one but two goats, as well as three flocks of chicks.

A Tree Grows in Texas

St. John Vianney Parish in Round Rock, Texas, is a new church that was built just over a year ago. Baby trees were planted around the church to provide shade and beauty. But in Texas, where it's hot and dry for much of the year, little trees will die if they're not watered and cared for. Allison Tischler, seven, and her little sister, Chanelle, five, gave drink to the thirsty trees for nearly a year by visiting the parish every week to water the baby trees. The girls and their parents, along with three other families from the church, spent at least an hour every week, dragging the hose out, moving the mulch around the trees, watering the saplings, and then replacing the mulch so the water could soak into the roots.

Thanks to the girls, the young trees grew and grew, and are now a healthy, beautiful part of the parish's landscape. The trees also provide shade, a place for birds to nest, and oxygen for people to breathe. Caring for trees is one way to thank God for his gift of nature.

Idea Starters

Who is thirsty? Many people are thirsty for a refreshing drink. Find out who they are and what they need to quench their thirst. The students at Nativity School in Charleston, South Carolina, buy bottled water to hand out to migrant workers who are working out in the hot sun. The Boy Scouts of Troop 111 in Lansing, Michigan, give water bottles to people walking in the annual National Kidney Foundation walk/run in Lansing. Could you donate formula for babies to a pregnancy center or women's shelter? How about cans or bottles of juice for your neighborhood food pantry? Does a soup kitchen need coffee or hot chocolate to serve along with dinners on cold winter days?

Work together to bring drink to the thirsty. Some projects—building a well in an African village, buying goats for a family in Haiti—take more resources than just one kid usually has. But if you work together with a group of friends, classmates, or parishioners, you can come up with some creative and fun ways to raise money. Then you can make a donation to a group like Ryan's Well or Heifer International. Maybe you could set up a "wishing well" at school where students can toss their change to raise money for a well. Maybe you could sell stuffed animals (cows, goats, llamas) to earn enough to buy a milk-producing animal through Heifer. People might pay to hear a speaker or watch a video about the work being done by your favorite charity to provide clean water or milk to those who need it. Of course, there's always the tried-and-true lemonade stand—your customers get a drink and also help you raise money to give drink to others!

Take care of the water we have. In order for the world's people to have clean water, everyone has to work together to conserve water and make sure that it's clean. Try not to take water for granted. You can conserve water by remembering to turn off the faucet while you brush your teeth, by taking shorter showers, and by running appliances like the dishwasher and the washing machine only when they are full. Encourage others to do the same. Do what you can to help keep the lakes, rivers, and streams in your community clean. Adopt a section of a river and help clean up any trash and junk that's polluting the area. Write a letter to the editor of your local paper asking people to dispose of chemicals and trash properly so that waterways are not contaminated. Celebrate Earth Day (April 22) by making posters showing how people can take care of the planet.

STEWARDSHIP PRAYER
Giving Drink to the Thirsty

Dear Jesus,
You said that you are the living water and that those who believe in you will never thirst. Help us bring refreshing water to those who are thirsty. Help us care for the gifts of the earth, so that all living creatures can enjoy clean water. Amen.

Chapter 4

Kids Can...Welcome the Stranger

Do not neglect to show hospitality to strangers, for by doing that some have entertained angels without knowing it. —Hebrews 13:2

In the Old Testament, Abraham and Sarah were kind to a group of strangers who showed up at their tent. They welcomed them and gave them a meal. In return for their kindness, the strangers (who were really angels) granted them blessings from God—a baby, and a promise that their family would be blessed forever. Throughout the Bible, God's chosen people knew what it was

READ ALL ABOUT IT · READ ALL ABOUT IT · READ ALL ABOUT IT · READ ALL ABOUT IT ·

You can read the story of Abraham and Sarah in Genesis 18:1–9; and about Mary and Joseph in Luke 2:1–7 and Matthew 2:13–15.

like to be strangers—as slaves in Egypt, as wanderers in the desert, and as exiles under conquering kings.

Even Jesus' family knew what it was like to be strangers. When Mary and Joseph knocked on door after door in Bethlehem, trying to find a place to spend the night, they knew what it was like to be rejected. They also felt the welcome of the innkeeper who let them use his stable as a place to have their baby. Later, when the Holy Family fled to Egypt to escape from Herod's men who wanted to kill baby Jesus, they were strangers in a foreign country. Because God's people have so often been strangers, God asks us to treat the strangers we meet with caring and compassion.

Who is a stranger? A stranger is someone we do not know. A stranger could be someone who is different from us—a person from another country, someone who speaks a different language, has skin that is a different color, wears unusual clothing, or whose beliefs are different from ours. A stranger might be the new kid in your class, the family that moved into the house across the street, the refugee from Africa, the child in a foster home, or the migrant worker who is harvesting crops at a farm outside of town.

In a way, though, none of these people should be strangers to us. They are all God's children, which makes them our brothers and sisters. Even more than that, Jesus says that when we welcome the stranger, we welcome him. Who wouldn't want to welcome Jesus to their home, their school, or their church? Some people

A NOTE TO PARENTS, TEACHERS, AND CATECHISTS • A NOTE TO PARENTS, TEACHERS, AND CATECHISTS •

Protecting our children is vitally important in today's world. While we would like to believe that a stranger is Jesus in disguise, the truth is that sometimes a stranger may actually be danger in disguise. Work with your child to find ways to be welcoming and still stay safe.

say, "A stranger is a friend you haven't met yet." Or you might think of a stranger as a gift that's been wrapped in unusual paper. You're not sure what the gift is, but it will be fun to discover what's inside.

You may be thinking, "My parents told me not to talk to strangers! Strangers can be dangerous." Of course, Jesus doesn't want you to be in danger. Your parents, teachers, and other trusted adults in your life can help you identify the strangers in your world whom you can welcome as Jesus wants you to. They can help you by telling you which strangers are all right to approach and the best ways to serve them. Using common sense, always having at least two people working together, and always having an adult who knows what you are doing will help you to be safe while still carrying out the call of the gospel.

Can-Do Kids

Meet some kids who are heeding the call to welcome the stranger—Adam Rene and Alex, Nicole and Zack, and Makenzie.

Books and Toys Bring Smiles to Migrant Kids

Adam Rene Rosenbaum, nine, and his little brother Alex, six, liked to go with their mom and dad to visit migrant camps in northern Michigan. Migrant workers travel from place to place to find work planting and harvesting crops. They can be found in most areas of the country. Adam Rene and Alex's father, who grew up as a migrant worker, is now a college professor who volunteers his time helping migrant workers. Adam Rene and Alex enjoyed meeting the migrant worker's children, but saw that they had no toys to play with or books to read. Instead of being sad, though, Adam Rene decided to do something to help.

"I knew that soccer was a big thing in Texas and Mexico, where many of these kids come from. More than one child at a time can play with a soccer ball, so I got the idea of collecting soccer balls for the migrant kids," he said. He asked his pastor at St. Joseph Parish in St.

Johns, Michigan, if he could put a basket in the back of the church where people could donate soccer balls. Then he and his family called and emailed people to let them know what they were doing. They collected 100 soccer balls, which were sent to migrant camps.

That fall, when Adam Rene's little brother was learning to read, his parents told him, "Once you learn to read, you can do anything." They told the boys that education helped their dad leave the migrant life and make a better living for himself and his family. Adam Rene remembered that the migrant kids he had met didn't have any books. So he and his brother started the Clinton County Michigan Migrants Book Drive as a service project at their parish school. They asked people to donate new or used children's books, bilingual (English and Spanish) books, and Christian books. In nine months, the boys collected more than 4,000 books. Other people donated rosaries, board games, backpacks, and school supplies to give to the migrant children.

Adam Rene and Alex sorted the books by age level and helped hand out the books to the children. Adam Rene and Alex read to the children and told them that they could keep the books.

"It was great to see the looks on their faces when they realized the books were theirs to keep," said Adam Rene. "I like serving others as Jesus did. It makes me feel good inside."

Growing a Friendship Garden

Immigrants and refugees are people who have left their home country to find a new life in another country. Refugees leave their country because they have no home left, either because of war or natural disasters like earthquakes or floods. The African country of Sudan has been at war for many years. Families have been torn apart when mothers and fathers were killed and their children left as orphans. Thousands of Sudanese orphans have come to the United States to start a new life. Two of these Sudanese children, Eldura and Rosa, had to flee their villages when they were children. They grew up in a refugee camp without their families for eleven years. There they fell in love, got married, and had three children. In 2001, they were able to move to America and settled in Idaho. Soon they met the Gomolski family and became friends.

Darci Gomolski helped Eldura and Rosa learn to speak English and showed them how to find their way around in the community. The children of the two families became friends. When nine-year-old Nicole Gomolski and her seven-year-old brother, Zack, planted a garden last year, they decided to plant okra and pumpkins. These were not the children's favorite foods, but they were favorites of Eldura and Rosa, who remembered growing the vegetables back in Africa.

"Eldura showed Nicole a good way to plant and how to care for the crops," said Darci. "At harvest time, Nicole brought bags of okra to Rosa and Eldura. When Zack gave Eldura the first pumpkin from his harvest, Rosa called their Sudanese friends to come and share the bounty with them."

Zack wasn't sure at first whether he wanted to share too many of his pumpkins, but he changed his mind when he saw the joy that these gifts brought to their new friends. After all, he was just planning to make jack-o'-lanterns from them, but Eldura and Rosa used them for food. "The light in Eldura's eyes when he looks at our garden is pure happiness for us," said Darci. "The kids can't wait to plant another garden to share with others."

A Bag of Their Own

Foster children are kids who live with other families either because their own parents have died or because the parents are not able to take care of them. Many times, foster children are moved from house to house; they know what it's like to be a stranger over and over again. When they move, they often carry their belongings in a trash bag.

When seven-year-old Makenzie Snyder of Bowie, Maryland,

learned that foster kids had only trash bags to keep their stuff in, she wanted to do something about it. Even though she was only in the second grade at St. Pius X Regional School, she knew she had to help. She called friends and asked them to donate suitcases and duffel bags so that foster kids could have luggage of their own. She calls her project Children to Children, and has donated thousands of bags to foster kids in Maryland and Washington, D.C.

Now thirteen, Makenzie is still collecting duffel bags and giving them away. She includes a stuffed animal in each bag, so that the child who receives it will have a special friend to take with them wherever they go. She also includes a note that reads:

"God told me you could use a duffel bag and a cuddly friend. So I send this with love to you. I want you to always know that you are loved, especially by me. Always remember to be positive, polite, and never give up. Love, your friend, Makenzie."

Makenzie has a website, www.childrentochildren.org, that includes information on how others can make donations of stuffed animals, suitcases, and duffel bags. It even tells how to hold a duffel bag drive in their own community. "I like to do this because these kids need me," she said.

Idea Starters

Find out what it means to be a stranger. One of the first steps toward welcoming strangers is understanding who strangers are and how they feel. Two good books that tell about strangers at school are *The Brand New Kid*, by Katie Couric, and *The Hundred Dresses*, by Eleanor Estes. Both are stories about kids from other countries who come to new schools, and how they are treated by their classmates. You might want to talk with your family or school friends about the books and about how you treat new children at your school. How can you make sure that new kids feel welcome?

What do strangers need to feel welcome? When you welcome the stranger, you make them feel comfortable and "at home." How can you do this? A friendly smile and greeting go a long way to making someone feel welcome. When you see someone new at school, at church, or in your neighborhood, say hello. Take some time to learn a little bit about the new person. Your parish may have a hospitality ministry that welcomes new people. Ask if they need help putting together welcome packets for new parishioners at your church. You can also ask your teacher, principal, or guidance counselor at school what you can do to help welcome new students.

Celebrate how we are alike and how we are different. One of the best ways for people to stop being strangers is to learn about each other. One way that you can be welcoming is to ask the strangers at your church or school to share with you some of their traditions, customs, special foods, or music. You can also share your traditions, customs, food, and music with them. Suggest that your class celebrate a "culture day" where everyone brings in something from their ethnic tradition to share with one another. Maybe your parish can find a way to include songs in other languages at Mass to make people from other countries feel welcome. You may discover that you have more in common than you thought. Everyone will learn to appreciate one another a little bit more.

For more ideas, see "Stewardship Resources," in Chapter 9.

STEWARDSHIP PRAYER
Welcoming the Stranger

Dear God,
All people on earth are your children. Help us see our brothers and sisters in the face of every stranger we meet. Teach us to welcome them as we would welcome our brother, Jesus. We ask this in his name. Amen.

Chapter 5

Kids Can...
Clothe the Naked

In reply Jesus said to them, "Whoever has two coats must share with anyone who has none; and whoever has food must do likewise." —Luke 3:11

Everyone comes into this world without any clothing, but we don't stay that way for long. Babies are wrapped in blankets. Moms and dads (and grandmas and grandpas) buy cute little outfits for the new baby. Friends and relatives make or buy clothes, blankets, and afghans for baby to snuggle in. It's their way of showing how much this baby is loved.

As we grow, clothing means a lot. Whether it's a special Christmas dress, a First Communion suit, or new jeans for the first day of school, we all have clothes that remind us of special times in our lives. Even our everyday clothes mean a lot to us—a comfy pair of sweats, the sneakers that help us run faster than anyone else on the playground, the flannel pajamas that are just perfect for chilly winter nights. Clothing is useful, too. Shoes protect our feet from rocks and hot pavement, shirts and pants block the sun's rays and the wind's chill, and coats and hats keep us warm and dry.

Many people don't have a choice about what they are going to wear. They may only have one or two outfits, or even just the clothes on their backs. They may have to wear shoes that are too small because new shoes cost too much. They may stand out in the cold with their hands in their pockets because they have no coat and no gloves to keep them warm. They may feel sad or embarrassed because they don't have the same kind of clothes other people do.

Clothes do more than protect our bodies. They also help us express who we are. There's an old saying, "Don't judge a book by its cover." Yet, people look at our clothes to find out something about us. Some people only want to wear clothes with designer labels, or they have to have the latest fashion. Others have a special color or style they like to wear. Clothing can be fun as well as useful. Clothes can make us feel good.

When we follow Christ's command to clothe the naked, we do two things at once. We are clothing people's bodies, but we are also clothing their dignity. Persons feel good about themselves when they have clothes that fit, that keep them warm, and that look well on them.

The Bible has many examples of giving clothing to those who need it. In the story of the Prodigal Son, the young man's father brings him a new robe to replace the rags he is wearing. Jesus told his followers if they have two coats, to give one away to someone who has no coat at all. St. James wrote that it does no good to tell someone to keep warm and well if you do not also give them

READ ALL ABOUT IT · READ ALL ABOUT IT · READ ALL ABOUT IT · READ ALL ABOUT IT ·

The prodigal son is a story of love and forgiveness shown by a father to his child. Read the story in Luke 15:11–32. St. James tells his readers that their faith must be seen through good works (James 2:14–17). Talk with someone about how you can show your faith in action.

clothing so they can keep warm. The Bible also tells us about another kind of clothing that we should wear—the invisible clothing that shows we are Christians. "As God's chosen ones, holy and beloved, clothe yourselves with compassion, kindness, humility, meekness, and patience…. Above all, clothe yourselves with love" (Colossians 3:12–14).

Can-Do Kids

If God has blessed us with the gift of having enough clothes to wear, then we must, as his stewards, share those gifts with others. Here are some kids who are following Jesus' call to clothe the naked.

Winter Warmth Begins with Mittens, Coats, and Loving Hearts

For the past three years, sisters Kristina and Liza Giangrande of Andover, Massachusetts, have tried to make the cold New England winters a little warmer for children in the nearby town of Lawrence. With their Winter Warmth Project, the eleven- and eight-year-old girls have collected hats, mittens, coats, and other winter clothing to give to needy grade school students.

The Giangrande sisters attend St. Augustine Parish, which supports Lazarus House, a soup kitchen and homeless shelter in Lawrence. About five years ago, the Giangrande family decided to donate food and clothing to Lazarus House instead of giving birthday presents to their kids, who also include six-year-old Peter and three-year-old Jason. Three years ago, when Kristina's birthday came, she and her family got a tour of the homeless shelter after they dropped off their gifts of clothing. The children were stunned by what they saw.

"Is that really everything they own in that one clothes basket?" Kristina asked her mother. "They had maybe one piece of clothing for each kid," she recalled. "I felt bad for the people who had to stay in those rooms." At first, Kristina wanted to give tents and blankets to the poor people in Lawrence. That way, they could be warm and also have a place of their own to stay. She researched information about poverty in Lawrence. Kristina learned that seventy-two percent—almost three-quarters—of the families in Lawrence are poor. She wrote a letter to the mayor telling her about her idea. The mayor thanked Kristina, but explained that there was no space to pitch all those tents. Instead, the mayor asked her to collect hats and mittens for the poor.

So Kristina and Liza did just that. They held a bake sale and raffles and raised enough money to give 400 sets of hats and mittens to needy children. The next year they decided to add boots and coats. They wrote to clothing manufacturers to ask for donations. How happy they were when companies like Land's End, New Balance, One Step Ahead, and Stride Rite came through for them!

Kristina and Liza don't just collect any old coats to give to kids, though. They ask school counselors to find specific children who need coats, and then they go out and buy new ones in the right sizes for each child. So six-year-old Martha gets a new coat, and eleven-year-old Henry gets a new coat, each picked out and gift-wrapped just for them. This winter, the Winter Warmth Project gave 385 new coats to children who needed them.

Kristina and Liza's mother, Karen Giangrande, said that the girls' project works because of "God's grace and his direction.... We know that God is in the middle and we're just along for the ride," she said.

Coats Can Make a Difference

Cecilia Cruz, an eleven-year-old in Salinas, California, read in her Sunday newspaper about "Make a Difference Day." This Day is a national program held every October as a way to motivate people throughout the United States to help others in their community. Cecilia decided she would collect coats for the homeless. In the two weeks before Make a Difference Day, Cecilia obtained forty coats which she donated to Dorothy's Place, a homeless shelter run by the Franciscans in Salinas.

"It's something good for me to do," said Cecilia. "Now that I'm older, I notice other people's needs. God says we can't only keep things to ourselves, but we have to give to others, like the homeless."

For the next year Cecilia decided she wanted to collect 100 coats for Make a Difference Day. But no matter how many coats she gathers, she's happy to help someone who needs it. "When you give, you just give from your heart," she said.

Idea Starters

Charity begins at home. Take a look in your closet. Have you and your family been blessed with lots of clothing? Do you really need all those clothes? A good project to do at least once a year is to sort through your clothing. Collect anything you've outgrown or no longer wear. Donate what you've gathered to a group that gives or resells clothing to people who might not be able to afford new things. Some of these groups are Goodwill Industries, St. Vincent de Paul Society, your local Catholic Charities, the Salvation Army, and Volunteers of America. Your diocese, parish, or community may also have a ministry that provides clothing to those in need.

Who needs clothing? Ask your parents, teachers, or someone at your parish to help you figure out where the need for clothing is the greatest. In the winter, your church or school might sponsor a mitten tree or collect hats and scarves to help others keep warm. People in nursing homes and hospitals might need lap robes and blankets to keep them from being chilly. A local pregnancy center that helps women who are having babies might need diapers, blankets, and baby clothes. Women and children who have left a bad home situation and are staying in a shelter may have only the clothes they were wearing when they left. The Red Cross helps people whose homes have been destroyed by fire or other disasters. These folks need clothes, too.

At the start of a new school year, some families may not be able to afford new school clothes for their children. Some groups collect money and take kids on a shopping trip to pick out some new clothes and shoes for school. A fun way to help another child who needs new school clothes is to imagine that you have a twin somewhere in the world. When you buy a new outfit for school, purchase (or ask your family to purchase) a second outfit for your "twin," then give it to an organization that is helping needy kids get new school clothes. After all, if you like the clothes you picked out, so would someone else your age.

Use your talents in the service of others. Do you know how to knit, crochet, or quilt? You can use those talents to make afghans or blankets for babies, people in hospitals, or seniors in nursing homes. You could make mittens, hats, or scarves to keep people warm. One girl in New York named Shifra visited a soup kitchen with a group of classmates to serve dinner to the homeless. Shifra saw that many of the people there had clothing that was torn or missing buttons. Since she knew how to sew, she offered to come back to the shelter and repair clothing. Six years later, Shifra is still volunteering at the soup kitchen, replacing lost buttons, stitching up torn pockets, and fixing holes in pants and coats. She found a way to use the gifts God gave her to help others. Think about what you can do that could help clothe the naked.

For more "Stewardship Resources," see Chapter 9.

STEWARDSHIP PRAYER
Clothe the Naked

Heavenly Father,
You clothe us with your love every day. Help us be aware of the needs of others. Teach us to share what we have with those who do not have enough. We ask this in Jesus' name. Amen.

Chapter 6

Kids Can...
Comfort the Sick

As the sun was setting, all those who had any who were sick with various kinds of diseases brought them to him; and he laid his hands on each of them and cured them.
—Luke 4:40

Jesus healed a lot of sick people during his time on earth. In the Bible, when Jesus touched someone who was ill, they could see, or hear, or walk again. Not only did they feel better, their sadness was changed to happiness at being well. When we comfort the sick, we may not be able to heal them the way Jesus did. However, we can make them feel better by our caring and compassion. That may be just as important as physical healing.

It's no fun to be sick. Think back to a time when you were sick—maybe you had a bad cold, a stomachache, a sore throat, or even a broken leg. Doctors and medicine might have helped the aches and pain, but what really made you feel better? It was probably the comfort you received from someone who loved you. Did your mom make warm ginger ale to calm your stomach? Did your dad bring home your favorite flavor of ice cream for your sore throat? Did you get to wrap up in a special blanket on the couch and watch a video? Maybe your parents read to you or played soft music to help you sleep. Perhaps your classmates made get-well cards and dropped them off at your house along with the homework you missed. The warm, loved feeling you experienced at those times was "comfort."

READ ALL ABOUT IT · READ ALL ABOUT IT · READ ALL ABOUT IT · READ ALL ABOUT IT

There are many, many stories in the Bible about Jesus healing people. Here are just a few for you to read. Which is your favorite?

Matthew 8:1–17
Matthew 8:27–32
Mark 8:22–26
Luke 17:11–19
John 9:1–12

When we comfort those who are sick, we mirror God's love for us. Our actions help God to be present to the sick person. We show them a glimpse of what God's great love is like. In a way, we become God's hands, reaching out to that person and giving them God's comfort.

In the days when Jesus was ministering on earth, many people thought that sickness was a sign someone was being punished for sin. If you tried to help that person, it was as though you were saying it was okay the person had sinned. But Jesus told people that, as his followers, they should help those who were sick. Jesus showed people that sickness was not a punishment for sin. He told them that God did not ignore those who were sick or injured and neither should God's followers.

Today, we know that sickness doesn't mean that someone is a bad person. Yet, many times sick people feel rejected by others. People stay away, either because they are afraid of becoming sick or because they don't know how to help. When we remember Jesus' call to comfort the sick, we get over our fears and our feeling of helplessness so we can be there for someone who really needs us.

Can-Do Kids

Kids can comfort the sick in many ways. Learn how Stephanie, Kristen and Leah, and Jamie used their gifts to answer the call to comfort the sick.

Puppy Love for Sick Kids

Stephanie Garcia loves dogs. This eighth-grader from Louisville, Kentucky, has been active in her local 4-H club, raising money to provide police dogs with bulletproof vests. She also works with people who do pet therapy at local hospitals and children's homes. These people bring dogs to visit sick and lonely children to cheer them up and give them some "puppy love." Stephanie thought that kids might be sad when their pet therapy visit was over. So she started "Little Heroes," a project that provides stuffed dogs as part of pet therapy visits.

WAGS, a Louisville pet therapy group that visits children at Kosair's Children's Hospital and the Home of the Innocents, works with Stephanie, who gives the volunteers the stuffed dogs to give to children as a reminder of their visit.

"This way the kids will have their own Little Hero," Stephanie explained. "Later on, if they are afraid, or lonely, or don't feel good, they can have this new friend to hold on to. I hope it will cheer them up."

How "Can" We Help?

When Leah Root's friend, Emily, suffered from a bad illness and had to be in a special hospital far from her home in Hudson Falls, New York, Leah wondered how to help her friend's family. Seven-year-old Leah and her older sister, Kristen, eleven, were worried because Emily's parents had to drive back and forth from the hospital, and the price of gas was very high.

The girls decided to raise some money by collecting soda cans and taking them to the recycling center. Kristen and Leah made a flier that they delivered house to house and gave to friends in their religious education classes at St. Mary/St. Paul Parish. In a week, they had made $114, and in another week, they raised another $211.

Then a radio DJ learned about what the girls were doing when his son brought home one of the fliers from religious education class. The DJ told about the sisters' soda can drive on the air, telling listeners to bring their cans to the church parking lot the following week. Everyone was surprised by the traffic jam of people bringing their cans to help out. Emily's father, who is a police officer, directed traffic. A group of Boy Scouts helped to sort cans, and Leah collected donations of loose change. When they were done, they had collected 15,000 cans and raised more than $2,000.

Emily's family was comforted by Kristen and Leah's concern. They were able to visit their daughter without worrying about paying for gas to make the trip to the hospital.

Heads Up for Cancer Research

Kids with cancer have to deal with a lot. They miss school because they are sick, they are tired out from medical treatments, and, a lot of times, they lose their hair! Jamie Deibel, a student at St. Albert School in Louisville, Kentucky, knows just how it feels to be a kid with cancer. In September 2001, she was diagnosed with leukemia, a kind of cancer that often affects children. But she didn't spend a lot of time feeling sorry for herself. Instead, she found a way to help herself and other kids with cancer.

Jamie heard about St. Baldrick's Day, a fund-raising event sponsored by the National Childhood Cancer Foundation. Jamie asked if her school would like to join. St. Baldrick is an imaginary saint who has a bald head, just like many kids with cancer. On St. Baldrick's Day, which is the same day as St. Patrick's Day, people raise awareness about cancer by shaving their heads in return for donations of money. Jamie's principal liked the idea, so on March 17, 2003, St. Albert the Great Parochial School celebrated St. Baldrick's Day.

Sixty-five boys from the school shaved their heads to show support for Jamie and other children who have lost their hair from chemotherapy. Sixteen girls donated six or more inches of their hair to Locks of Love, an organization that makes wigs for children who have lost their hair. St. Albert's was the largest school in the United States to participate in St. Baldrick's Day, raising $6,500 for the National Childhood Cancer Foundation.

Idea Starters

You may think, "I don't want to be around sick people. I might get what they have." But as the stories of these "can-do kids" show, you don't have to be physically present to someone in order to comfort them, although visiting a sick person can be very comforting to them. What are some ways you can comfort the sick?

Do you know someone who is sick? If a family member is sick, you can comfort them by helping around the house, bringing them things they need to feel better (a drink, something to eat, tissues, a blanket), reading to them, or doing some of the things they usually take care of. If a friend or classmate is sick, you can make them a get-well card, send them a book or toy, or call them on the phone (or send an e-mail) to let them know that you are thinking about them.

Pray for the sick. Your parish has a list of people in your church who are sick. You may hear their names during the Prayers of the Faithful during Mass, or they may be listed in the bulletin or a book of prayer intentions. Even if you don't know them personally, you can pray for them to get well or to be comforted in their illness. You can also pray for their families and the others (doctors, nurses, other health care workers) who take care of them.

Help those who help the sick. Even if you don't know anyone who is sick, you can assist others who are caring for the sick. Does your hospital have a pediatric (children's) wing? They might need books and toys to keep the young patients happy while they are in the hospital. Jarrett Mynear, a boy in Nicholasville, Kentucky, enjoyed playing with toys that volunteers brought him when he was in the hospital for cancer treatments. He decided to help other kids by starting Jarrett's Joy Cart, a program to give new toys to children in the hospital so they wouldn't feel so scared and lonely. He started the first Joy Cart at the University of Kentucky Children's Hospital in 1999. Before he died at age thirteen in October 2003, Jarrett had helped to get other Joy Carts started at hospitals in Illinois, Florida, and Washington. His website, www.thejoycart.com, tells how to bring a Joy Cart to a hospital in your community.

Some cities have a Ronald McDonald House or other place where families can stay when their child is in the hospital far from home. You can help comfort the families staying at a house like this by donating toys, food, or household products that will make their stay more home-like. Many Ronald McDonald Houses also accept donations of pop tabs that are recycled for money. Since 1987, over 400 million pop tabs have been collected, raising $300,000. You might suggest to your family, class, or parish that collecting pop tabs would be a good way to comfort the sick and their families.

Other ways to comfort the sick include drawing pictures or sending cards to people in the hospital or in nursing homes. You could also record your favorite stories on tape for a sick person to listen to.

Help find a cure. One way to comfort the sick is to try to end sickness in the world. If someone you know has been touched in any way by a disease, you may be able to donate money to an organization that is trying to find a cure for that disease. Or you can

A NOTE TO PARENTS, TEACHERS, AND CATECHISTS • A NOTE TO PARENTS, TEACHERS, AND CATECHISTS •

Make a point of including prayers for the sick and those who care for them in your shared prayers. Encourage your child to pray for friends who are absent from school or for family members who are ill. If you don't already do so, you might want to start a family custom of saying a brief prayer whenever an ambulance drives past.

sign up for an event like a walkathon to raise money for a cause. The St. Jude Center for Children, American Heart Association, the American Cancer Society, the American Diabetes Association, the National Kidney Foundation, the March of Dimes, and the National Childhood Cancer Foundation are some examples of groups that hold fundraising events.

For additional ideas, see Chapter 9, "Stewardship Resources."

STEWARDSHIP PRAYER
Comforting the Sick

Dear Jesus,
Your touch healed the sick and gave them new life. Teach us to be your hands, touching those who are sick with care and compassion. Show us how to be healers wherever we see sadness, pain, and suffering. We ask this in your name. Amen.

Chapter 7

Kids Can...
Visit the Imprisoned

Remember those who are in prison, as though you were in prison with them.
—Hebrews 13:3

Jesus said that he came to set the captives free and to preach the good news to prisoners. He also said that those who visit people in prison are really visiting him. This may be the most difficult work of mercy that Jesus asks his followers to do. For kids especially, visiting prisoners requires creativity, because kids are not allowed into prisons.

Why should we visit prisoners, anyway? After all, they've committed crimes—they're bad people who can never be saved, right? Wrong! Prisoners may have done bad things, but that does not make them bad people. All people, no matter what side of the prison bars they are on, are still children of God. They still can go to heaven if they repent. They deserve our care, our prayers, and compassion. As Christians, we believe in the power of God's love, mercy, and forgiveness. In the Lord's Prayer, we pray, "Forgive us our trespasses as we forgive those who trespass against us." If we really believe that, we need to show forgiveness even to those in prison. Forgiving someone doesn't mean that

A NOTE TO PARENTS, TEACHERS, AND CATECHISTS • A NOTE TO PARENTS, TEACHERS, AND CATECHISTS •

Be certain to read any card or letter that a child writes to a prisoner to ensure that no identifying information is given accidentally. Talk with your child to make sure they understand that, even though a prisoner is paying for his or her crime, he or she is still a child of God who deserves our prayers.

what they did was all right, or that they don't have to make up for what they did. But while they are in prison for their crimes, they still need to know that God loves them and that people care about them.

As Christians, we also believe that God can change people's hearts. Even people who have made serious mistakes can turn their lives around with God's help. By ministering to prisoners, we give people a reason to turn back to God by sharing God's love.

Just as with the call to welcome the stranger, visiting the imprisoned must be approached with common sense and caution, especially for kids. God doesn't want you to put yourself in danger. Always work with an adult on any project that involves contact with prisoners. When you write to prisoners, never give any information that would identify you, such as your last name, your address, your school, and so on. Use only your first name. Keep the subjects you are writing about focused on God's love and care and Christ's message of forgiveness. Prayer cards, artwork, and simple gifts are best.

Can-Do Kids

Children in South Carolina, New York, and Missouri know what it's like to reach out to those who are in prison. Here are their stories.

A Love Letter from One Child of God to Another

Fourth-graders at Nativity School in Charleston, South Carolina, write letters to inmates at prisons in the Charleston area. Mimi Jurgielewicz, director of social justice programs at the school, teaches her students that it doesn't matter why a person is in prison. What matters is that they are God's children.

"What we look at is that this is a child of God, related to us through baptism. We're not here to judge or to question, but to bring them Christ's greetings, to let them know that God loves them," she explained. The students' letters to the inmates begin, "Dear Child of God." In the letters, the children let the prisoners know about Christ's unconditional love and forgiveness. They share Scripture passages with them and let them know that someone is thinking about them. During the school year, the fourth-graders also pray for the prisoners and their families.

Ms. Jurgielewicz invites friends of hers who work in prison ministry to talk to the students about what they do. They share with the kids how they begin to see Christ in the prisoners as they minister to them. Another friend who works in prison ministry takes the letters from the students and delivers them to prisoners at one or more of the three prisons in the region.

"We don't know exactly who gets our letters, but that's not important," said Ms. Jurgielewicz. "What's important is that the children reach out to the inmates with a message of God's love, the way Jesus asked us to do."

A Colorful Easter Message of Hope

Students in the Mission Club at St. Paul's School in Kenmore, New York, make Easter cards and decorate candy bags that are given to 1,700 inmates at Attica Correctional Facility. Sister Karen Klimczak, director of HOPE Prison Ministries in the Diocese of Buffalo, noted that the prisoners are touched by the fact that the students have taken the time to create something handmade for them.

"When a child reaches out and shows that they care by coloring a picture, that means so much. Many of the inmates keep the bags and cards all year, using them to decorate their cells," she said. What do the prisoners think when they receive these gifts from Catholic school children? Here is what some of them had to say:

"As I looked into the bag among the refreshing delights, I found a little card with a crayon-colored bunny from a child. I was touched in such a special way. I just wanted to write and say thank you, not just for the bag but for the efforts spent to reach so many hearts with a special touch of genuine, God-felt love."

"At times when it seems like no one cares, you showed someone does. Thank you so much because it means a lot to a lonely human being such as myself."

"I got your Easter gift today. When I was young—around your age probably—I got wonderful baskets every Easter, filled with jellybeans and chocolate and marshmallow eggs. I am writing to tell you, though, that never in my life have I received one as beautiful as the one I got from you today…. Your message, 'It's spring!' gave me hope."

The students also get a lot out of "visiting" those in prison through their cards and artwork. twelve-year-old Maureen said, "I felt that these offenders should know that there are people in society who still care about them even though they made a mistake." Felix, thirteen, said that making a card made him think about the person who might receive his gift. "I remembered to pray for him," he said.

Reaching out to someone in prison isn't always easy. "At first it felt weird doing something nice for a criminal," said thirteen-year-old Andrew. "We were told that some inmates decorated their walls with the kids' artwork, so then I felt better about the project. I thought they might be depressed, and since they were paying for their crime, they deserved to be treated well."

Bringing Cheer In for Those Who Can't Go Out

Not every prison has bars, and not every prisoner is a criminal. For some people in nursing homes with a condition called Alzheimer's

Disease, the prison is their own mind. People with Alzheimer's Disease can't remember many of the things we take for granted: the names of loved ones, the faces of friends, the memories of good times, and sometimes even the knowledge of how to do everyday jobs like getting dressed and using a knife and fork. Because they can't remember how to get home again, many people with Alzheimer's live in nursing homes where medical professionals can take care of them and keep them safe.

Elizabeth Card, a fourteen-year-old student at St. Peter's Middle School in Joplin, Missouri, ministers to people with Alzheimer's Disease who live in a nursing home near her school. She started visiting the Greenbriar Home last summer as a volunteer job, and she loved it so much that her once a week visits soon grew to three times a week.

"I love being with these people and doing things with them," she said. "They're so nice, and they're always happy to see me, even if they don't remember who I am. Sometimes, someone will say, 'I know you. You went to my high school dance,' and I have to explain to them who I am. That can be a little sad, but I try to keep my spirits up so that they'll be happy."

Elizabeth brings patients from their rooms to the dining room and helps to feed those who need help. She chats with them, sings songs, plays games, and does arts and crafts. Every month, she comes to the home's birthday party for residents. She has even turned down paying babysitting jobs so that she can spend time with her friends at the nursing home.

"I help one lady who's blind to play bingo. Every week we try to win, but we never do. But we have so much fun trying," Elizabeth laughed.

Some day, Elizabeth would like to have a job where she can help people. For now, she plans to keep visiting the nursing home two or three times a week, sharing her smiles and laughter and time with her good friends.

Idea Starters

Learn about those who are in prison. Sister Anne Joseph Crookston, director of detention ministry in the Diocese of Orange, California, said that one in thirty-seven people has been in jail at some time. That's a lot of people. Some are in prison for serious crimes and others for not-so-serious reasons. Many of them came from homes where they were abused or did not have good role models. They have made bad choices in their lives. They are not evil people, but are people who have made mistakes. Other people are in jail because they broke a law while protesting something that they felt was unjust.

There are people in jail for peacefully protesting at abortion clinics, for protesting about the United States' military policies, and for speaking out against unjust conditions in the world. These people are "criminals" in the eyes of the government, but they are doing what they believe Jesus wants them to do, and for that, they are in jail.

READ ALL ABOUT IT • READ ALL ABOUT IT • READ ALL ABOUT IT • READ ALL ABOUT IT

Some of Jesus' followers ended up in prison for preaching about Jesus. In the Acts of the Apostles, you can read about how an angel freed the apostles after they had been put in jail (Acts 5:17-23). You can also read about how St. Paul had the chance to escape from prison and didn't (Acts 16:25–40).

Other people are in jail because they have broken laws about using or selling drugs or alcohol. Addiction to harmful substances like drugs and alcohol is another kind of imprisonment, even if a person isn't in jail.

Think about other ways that people are "in prison." Fred LaPuzza, coordinator for adult facilities for the Diocese of Orange, notes that people can be imprisoned in many ways. According to him, Mother Teresa of Calcutta often said that some people in the United States imprison themselves by refusing to reach out to other people. People with Alzheimer's Disease are imprisoned by a condition that takes away their memories. Some people have physical problems that take away their ability to move, or make it very difficult. These diseases, such as muscular dystrophy, multiple sclerosis, or ALS (Lou Gehrig's Disease), may imprison people within their own bodies, but their minds and hearts are still free. Other people may feel imprisoned by a lack of education or by poverty or poor living conditions.

What can you do to help? Even though you can't go and visit prisoners in jail, there are still many ways to minister to them and to their families. Some ideas include:

- collecting Bibles for distribution to inmates;
- making birthday cards for young people in juvenile detention facilities;
- hosting a holiday party for families and children of inmates;
- writing letters to those who are in prison;
- providing cards and stamps so that prisoners can write to their families;
- collecting toys and books that inmates can give to their children for Christmas;
- visiting people in hospitals or nursing homes;
- sending cards to shut-ins;
- providing food and clothing for the families of prisoners, who often are poor.

To learn more, see Chapter 9, "Stewardship Resources."

STEWARDSHIP PRAYER
Visiting the Imprisoned

Jesus Lord,
You said that you came to set the captives free. Help us share your Good News of God's love and mercy with those who are in prison. May we reach out to those who are in "prisons" of illness, addiction, and loneliness, and give them a taste of the freedom only you can give. Amen.

Chapter 8

Hey! Can My Mom and Dad Help, Too?

Share this chapter with your parents so they can learn about stewardship, too.

Moms and Dads, do you remember being commissioned by the Church to teach your children how to be good stewards? You were, you know, but you may not remember it because it wasn't put in just those words. Think back to your child's baptism, when you promised to raise your child in the practice of the faith. The baptismal rite says, "[Child's parents] will be the first teachers of their child in the ways of faith. May they also be the best of teachers, bearing witness to the faith by what they say and do, in Christ Jesus our Lord." These words are a call not only to teach our children to pray and attend Mass and learn about Jesus, but to teach them how to live a Christian life, including the practice of stewardship. When our actions show that we are grateful to God for what we have and we want to use those gifts to help others, our children learn what stewardship is and can begin to practice it.

An old saying states: "Tell me, I forget; show me, I remember; involve me, I understand." By involving our children, we help them understand the importance of stewardship and show them that it is a part of what we do as followers of Christ. It is not an extraordinary action, but simply one of the things we do because we are Christians. Whether it's giving your child the envelope to put into the Sunday collection, having her pick out the canned goods for the parish food drive, or bringing him along when you visit a friend or relative in a nursing home, you show your child that he or she is old enough to be an active Christian. Elizabeth Rusch, author of *Generation Fix: Young Ideas for a Better World,* found that children who are enthusiastic givers are usually from families in which the children's ideas are valued, and in which there is discussion about the world around them.

Most of the children featured in this book have parents who have encouraged a spirit of giving in their children by including them in their own charitable activities. The Rosenbaum family of St. Johns, Michigan, makes an annual family project of filling shoeboxes for poor children through Operation Christmas Child. They also took their boys with them when they visited migrant camps, which gave the boys the idea for their own stewardship initiative of collecting toys and books for migrant children. Madison Etzler's parents have included her in their family's philanthropic decisions since she was only a toddler, letting her choose the charities they would support, letting her pick out clothes to give to Goodwill, and selecting food for parish food drives. Now at the ripe old age of five, Madison is already an enthusiastic steward—because of her parents' example.

Sometimes, children can even teach parents a lesson in stewardship. Dreena Tischler of Austin, Texas, relates this story about her daughters, seven-year-old Allison and five-year-old Chanelle. "One day, while we were on an errand, we were at a stoplight and a lady was there with a sign, collecting money. The sign said, 'Working mother of two. Water cut off. Electricity's next. Please help.' It was over 100 degrees, and I was sitting at the light, sweating and thinking about our next errand. I read the sign but didn't even think about it. My five-year-old said, 'Mommy, what's she doing?' I told her she was poor and asking for money. My seven-year-old read her the sign, and my five-year-old said, 'Aren't we going to give her any money, Mom?' I honked my horn and dug out a couple of dollars—I NEVER have any cash—and felt very convicted by my kids! Right afterward, several people behind us honked and my older girl said, 'Look, Mom, we started a chain reaction.' Needless to say, I was crying as I drove on. How could I have become so numb? It could have been ME out there trying to protect my kids! That showed me how valuable children are in awakening the need for stewardship in adults."

Dreena Tischler knew what stewardship was, and practiced it with her children in many ways—helping to clean the church, watering baby trees on the church grounds, sending cards to seminarians—but it took her children to open her eyes to other opportunities for reaching out. They saw Christ in the face of a mother asking for help for her family and they acted on his words: "As much as you did it for the least of my brothers and sisters, you did it to me."

What are some ways you can instill and build a sense of stewardship in your children? Here are a few suggestions.

Make Them Aware of the Needs of Others

Most children would love to help others—they just need to know that there is a need. If our children are growing up in a loving home where their needs and wants are met, they may not realize that others do not have the same experience. I can remember when my oldest son was about six years old, he was helping me take a few canned goods to our mailbox for a U.S. Postal Service food drive. He asked me why we were doing this, and I explained that the food would go to feed poor people who were hungry. He asked if the poor people were far away in another country. When I told him no, the food was for people right in our city, he began to cry. "I didn't know there were hungry people here in Lansing," he said. "We should go and get a few more cans."

You may feel that your child isn't ready to know about the needs of others, that it's too sad and depressing to burden them with knowledge of poverty, hunger, sickness, loneliness, and the like. But children have large and loving hearts. Chances are, they won't feel defeated by the news that sorrow and poverty exist in the world. They'll want to do something about it. You can help them to make wise choices about how to help others.

Pray Together for the Needs of the World

Praying is an act of stewardship in which even the smallest child can participate. Praying helps us focus on the idea that everything we do is done with God's help and for God's glory. If you're not comfortable with making up a prayer, you can use the stewardship prayer in the first chapter of this book, or use one of the following suggestions.

- Pray the newspaper. Select stories in your daily paper and pray about the people and events there. For instance, "God, we ask you to bless the firefighters who are trying to put out the wildfires in California and keep them safe. Please watch over the people whose homes were burned in the fire and show us how we can help them." Or "God, the forecast says it's going to snow tonight. Please watch over those who have no shelter and no coats, and help us be generous givers to the rescue mission coat drive."

- Pray the bulletin. Look through your parish bulletin and pray for the success of the various projects going on in your church. "God, be with the confirmation students as they attend their retreat this Saturday. Help them to know you better." "God, thank you for the generous people in our parish who gave to the Thanksgiving food collection. Bless the people who gave the food and those who will receive it."

- Pray Matthew 25:34–40. Using the commands in Matthew 25, pray for the needs of the world. "God, help us see you in the faces of the sick. Help us comfort them by showing them your care and compassion." "God, forgive us for the times we have failed to see you hungry or thirsty. Help us reach out to others and share your good gifts with those in need."

Share Stories from the Bible and the Lives of the Saints

Give your children role models for stewardship. Bible stories such as the Good Samaritan, the Widow's Mite, and the Parable of the Talents can make good starting points for family discussions about how we serve God and one another. Your Catholic bookstore or parish school library should have a good selection of books or videos about saints who gave back to God with a grateful heart. Some good ones to look for include: St. Elizabeth of Hungary, St. Martin de Porres, St. Francis of Assisi, St. Katharine Drexel, St. Vincent de Paul, and St. Margaret of Scotland. And don't limit yourself to long-ago saints. Read together about "modern" saints such as Mother Teresa of Calcutta and the work she did among the poor in India, or Dorothy Day and the Catholic Worker movement. Surf the Internet together to find other stories about "stewardship saints."

Help Them Find Ways to Use Their Talents

Your children may say, "I don't have any talents," or "What can I do? I'm too young." Guide them in discovering the gifts that God has given them. They may think of "talents" as being big and impressive gifts, such as athletic ability, acting, singing, painting, or academic skills. Having a talent doesn't mean being the best at something but having the ability to do something. Help them see that their talents may also include being a good listener, making friends easily, getting along with others, being gentle with younger children, or being organized. Then guide them in deciding how they can use those talents to serve God and others.

Make Note of What Your Children Do

Children thrive on encouragement. When you see them performing loving actions and giving of their time, talent, and treasures—even in small ways—let them know that you appreciate what they are doing. Point out how much fun your daughter had when she invited the new girl at school over for a playdate (welcoming the stranger). Thank your son for bringing his brother a blanket when he was sick with a cold (comforting the sick). From these small steps, stewardship begins to grow.

Ask for Their Suggestions When You Are Making Decisions About How Your Family Will Share Its Money and Other Resources

Kids like to feel that they are part of the action and that they have valuable ideas to share. When you are deciding how you will share your resources, let them have a say in the decision. If you have decided to sponsor a child through a relief agency, perhaps your child can pick the country where your sponsored child will come from. Give your child options, such as "Should we bake cookies for the soup kitchen, stock shelves at the food pantry, or deliver meals to shut-ins as our way to feed the hungry?" "Shall we make a donation to Heifer International or Food for the Poor?" Your child may even be aware of other opportunities that you had not considered. They will be more likely to become enthusiastic stewards if they can help decide what to do.

Share Success Stories and Point Out Examples of How Stewardship Makes a Difference

Let your children know that their gifts of time, talent, and treasure are having an effect. It's easy for children to get discouraged if they can't see the results of their efforts. If your parish bulletin prints a message about the number of families who were served by the church's holiday food drive, share that information with your kids. If you read an article in the newspaper about how children at the hospital are enjoying the books and toys you helped to collect, clip the article and put it on your refrigerator. Go to the websites of charitable organizations that you support and show your children examples of the work they are doing with your donations.

Enlist the Help of Others

When the Church entrusted you with the task of rearing your children in the faith, it did not intend for you to go it alone. The Church has numerous resources for parents to help you as you bring up the young Christians in your care. Ask your pastor, director of religious education, or Catholic school principal for ideas about teaching your children about stewardship and for activities in which your family can reach out to others. Your parish may have a social justice ministry, stewardship committee, or chapter of the St. Vincent de Paul Society that can help you to make sense of what stewardship means and how you can practice it as a family. At the diocesan level, the office of stewardship and development, the Catholic education and formation office, and Catholic social service agencies such as Catholic Charities and Catholic Relief Services can provide you with helpful resources. All of these people and organizations are there to assist families as they grow in their faith.

For stewardship resources to share with your children, see Chapter 9.

STEWARDSHIP PRAYER
For Parents

Dear God,
You are a loving Father to us, your children. Help us as parents to guide our children in the practice of their faith so that they may grow in wisdom, understanding, and love. Help us model by our own actions the kind of active faith we want our children to learn. We ask this through Jesus Christ, your Son. Amen.

Stewardship Resources

Now that you know what stewardship is all about and have met other kids like you who are serving God by serving others, you may be inspired to find your own way of being an active steward. How do you begin? First, pray about what God might be asking you to do and how he wants you to serve him. Reflect on the gifts God has given you and decide how you can use them to say, "Thank you, God."

God has given you many people in your life who can provide guidance and direction. Your parents, school teachers, and religious education teachers may have ideas that will help you. Your pastor or parish social ministry team will be aware of opportunities to serve others. Ask them for ideas. At the diocesan level, the director of stewardship will be able to put you in touch with people and groups who can use your gifts.

Where to Find Ideas

Lots of organizations showcase the good things kids are doing to help others throughout the world. By writing to them or by visiting their website, you can learn about what other kids have done and get ideas for activities you can do.

Make a Difference Day

Not just for kids, the fourth Saturday in October is a national day for people to "make a difference" by helping others. Founded by *USA Weekend* magazine, hundreds of thousands of people and groups have made a difference in their communities. Their website includes an interactive "idea generator" to help you find a project that's just right for your interests and abilities.
www.makeadifferenceday.org

Kids Care Clubs

There are more than 800 Kids Care Clubs in all 50 states, made up of groups of kids who want to serve others. The goal of the clubs is to "develop compassion and the spirit of charity in children through hands-on service projects." Get ideas for projects, find a club near you, or learn how to start your own club.
www.kidscare.org or Kids Care Clubs, 975 Boston Post Rd., Darien, CT 06820

Kids Make a Difference

While this group is based in Los Angeles, California, their website has lots of great ideas that elementary and middle school kids can do.
www.kidsmakeadifference.org or Kids Make a Difference, PO Box 24922, Los Angeles, CA 90024

ZOOM Into Action

The popular PBS television show ZOOM has a special segment that highlights the good things kids are doing in their communities. Their website includes stories about how kids are ZOOMing into action, as well as a "How You Can Help" section to help you think of ways you might participate.
www.pbskids.org/zoom/action/

Catholic Agencies

The Catholic Church has many organizations dedicated to sharing the gospel and practicing the works of mercy, bringing Jesus' touch to a hurting world. The national offices of these groups can put you in touch with the local chapter in your diocese, and also provide you with ideas for sharing in their work.

Catholic Charities
www.catholiccharitiesusa.org
1731 King St., Alexandria, VA 22314

Catholic Relief Services
www.catholicrelief.org (click on the globe icon for their Kid's Page)
209 W. Fayette St., Baltimore, MD 21201

Society of St. Vincent de Paul
www.svdpusa.org
58 Progress Parkway, St. Louis, MO 63043

Food for the Poor
www.foodforthepoor.org
5505 W. 12th Ave., Dept. 9662, Deerfield Beach, FL 33442

Christian Foundation for Children and Aging
www.cfcausa.org
One Elmwood Ave., Kansas City, KS 66103

The Holy Childhood Association
Children helping children around the world. The USA branch is listed under the website of the Pontifical Missions.
www.holychildhoodusa.org
3329 Banforth Ave., Scarborough, Ontario, Canada M1L 4T3

National and International Agencies

These organizations provide clothing, food, housing assistance, disaster relief, and other support to people in need.

Heifer International
www.heifer.org
PO Box 8058, Little Rock, AR 72203

American Red Cross
www.redcross.org
2025 E St., NW, Washington, DC 20006

Save the Children
www.savethechildren.org
54 Wilton Rd., Westport, CT 06880

Volunteers of America
www.voa.org
1660 Duke St., Alexandria, VA 22314

Meals on Wheels
www.mowaa.org
1414 Prince St., Suite 302, Alexandria, VA 22314

Salvation Army
www.salvationarmyusa.org
615 Slaters Lane, Alexandria, VA 22313

Goodwill Industries
www.goodwill.org
9200 Rockville Pike, Bethesda, MD 20814

Organizations Started by Kids

Kids just like you have started organizations that help others. Some have started small and their actions have grown into something big. Learn more about what they are doing and how you can help.

Turkeys 4 America
Dan and Betsy Nally (Kids Can...Feed the Hungry) have pledged to end hunger one turkey at a time. Find out more about them here: www.turkeys4america.org

Ryan's Well Foundation
Ryan Hreljac (Kids Can...Give Drink to the Thirsty) wants to make sure that all of Africa has clean water. His story is here: www.ryanswell.org

Children to Children
Makenzie Snyder (Kids Can...Welcome the Stranger) is committed to providing duffel bags and stuffed animals to children in foster care. You can help, too.
www.childrentochildren.org

Free the Children
Craig Kielburger's organization, started when he was twelve years old, provides school supplies and health kits to children in developing countries and also works to bring peace through his program of children helping other children.
www.freethechildren.org

Read All about It

The following books and other publications may spark ideas for you, your family, and your parish. Some are available at bookstores or online; others may be available through your diocesan stewardship office.

The Kids' Guide to Service Projects: Over 500 Service Ideas for Young People Who Want to Make a Difference, by Barbara A. Lewis, ©1995, Free Spirit Books.

The Kids' Volunteering Book, by Arlene Erlbach, ©1998, Lerner Publication Co.

The Big Help Book: 365 Ways You Can Make a Difference by Volunteering, ©1994, Aladdin Library.

Volunteering to Help (Kids, in Your Neighborhood, the Environment, with Animals, Seniors, for a Political Campaign), ©2000, Children's Press.

The ABCs of Stewardship for Children and Youth, Archdiocese of Oklahoma City.

Good Things Are for Sharing: Curriculum Guide for Stewardship for Elementary School Level, Archdiocese of Louisville.

Youth Stewards in Formation, Diocese of Wichita.

Little Hands, Building Big, Archdiocese of Santa Fe.

Let the Children Come to Me, Diocese of Charlotte.

Stewardship Programs for Children and Youth, by Rita McCarthy Swartz, Sheed & Ward.

Teaching Our Youth to Share (booklet), by Msgr. Joseph Champlin, The Liturgical Press.

52 Ways to Teach Stewardship, by Nancy Williamson, ©1998, Rainbow Publishers.

Taking Care of God's Gifts: Stewardship, a Way of Life
Two booklets: for grades K-2 and grades 3-5, by Laurie A Whitfield, Our Sunday Visitor.

Introducing Catholic Social Teaching to Children with Stories and Activities, by Anne E. Neuberger, Twenty-Third Publications.